WHAT HAPPENED HERE?

VICTORIAN FACTORY

Marilyn Tolhurst
Photographs by Maggie Murray
Illustrations by Gillian Clements

Contents

A & C BLACK · LONDON

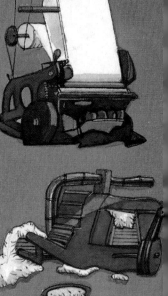

The factory

About two hundred years ago, a young man called Samuel Greg set out to explore the countryside around Manchester in search of a good place to build a water-powered cotton factory. At that time most spinning and weaving was done by hand in people's homes, but a surge of new inventions meant that it was suddenly possible to do the work with machines. This made the process of making cloth faster and cheaper. But the machines were large, and new factories or mills had to be built to house them.

Samuel Greg found a good spot for his cotton factory in a valley south of Manchester, where a fast-flowing river could be made to turn a waterwheel. This waterwheel would provide the power for his spinning machines. The factory was built in 1784. It was called Quarry Bank Mill. The factory grew to be enormously successful and the valley clattered with the noise of its machinery for the next 175 years.

The children in this book wanted to find out what it was like to live and work in a cotton factory in the past. They visited Quarry Bank Mill which is now a museum of the cotton industry. You can read what they found out in the following pages.

Samuel Greg
as a young man.

QUARRY BANK MILL

← to the
Apprentice house

This is how the factory looked in 1880 at the height of its success.

Arkwright's Spinning Frame. Richard Arkwright perfected the first water-powered spinning machine. It produced strong yarns. A version of this machine called the 'throstle' was used at Quarry Bank until 1856.

A cotton bale. Cotton was brought over from America in bales like this. It was cheap because it was picked by slaves in the great plantations of the American South.

to the Apprentices' Walk

the Manager's house

the waterwheel

the River Bollin

N

How do we know about the factory?

Quarry Bank Mill is a museum where visitors can absorb the sights, sounds and smells of a working cotton factory as it was 150 years ago. The children examined many different types of information that was gathered while the factory was being restored to working condition as a museum.

Documents
Huge leather-bound volumes of factory records still survive. These told the children a lot about factory life, including the type of machinery that was used and when it was repaired or changed; the names of the workers, and their hours and pay; the different types of jobs at the factory; accidents, stoppages and the ups and downs of trade.

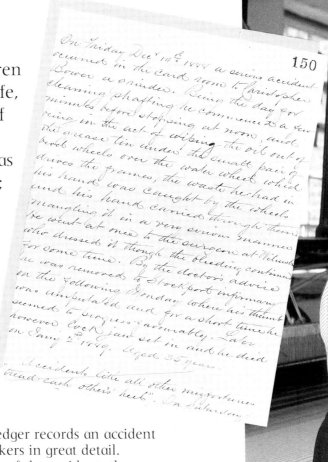

This page from the mill ledger records an accident to one of the factory workers in great detail. The report lists the causes of the accident, the treatment of the worker and his eventual death.

Pictures and photographs

Many illustrations survive which show us how cotton factories were arranged inside and how the machines were looked after. Later photographs give an even more accurate picture of factory life and work.

This photo shows us some of the factory girls who worked at Quarry Bank in the 1920s.

The children spoke to Mona Snape who was a power-loom weaver for many years. Nowadays she uses her experience to demonstrate weaving skills to visitors at Quarry Bank Mill.

Machinery

A great deal of early factory machinery still survives. Some of it has been restored and brought back to Quarry Bank so that people can see the machinery at work.

Memories

Many living people remember what it was like to work in a factory. Their memories and experiences, which sometimes go back several generations, give us valuable information about factory life in the past.

Time-lines

The first time-line shows some of the important dates in the history of cotton factories. The second time-line shows us some of the important events at Quarry Bank Mill up to the present day.

1764

Main events, ideas and inventions

1764 The Spinning Jenny was invented by James Hargreaves. This machine was operated by hand but could spin several threads at once.

1769 Richard Arkwright invented the Water Frame for spinning cotton. This used water as a source of power.

1779 Samuel Crompton invented the Spinning Mule which combined the movable frame of the Spinning Jenny with the water power of Arkwright's Frame.

1785 The first power-loom was invented and also the first cylinder printing machine for printing patterns on cloth.

1819 A Factory Act (a law passed by the government) made it illegal to employ children under 9 years of age in cotton factories.

1831 The Truck Act: all workers had to be paid in money and not in tokens that could only be used at factory shops where prices were high.

1784

Events at Quarry Bank Mill

1784 Quarry Bank Mill built by Samuel Greg, a young cloth merchant from Manchester.

1796 The mill was made bigger and a second waterwheel was added.

1818 A 100 horsepower suspension waterwheel, made by Thomas Hewes, was put in. New factory buildings were built over it.

1819 42 new workers' cottages were built in Styal village.

1823 A chapel, a school and a shop were opened in the village.

1834 Samuel Greg died aged 76. The factory was run by his son Robert Hyde Greg.

6

1833 A Factory Act laid down a 9-hour working day for children under 12 years of age. Child workers were to have two hours' schooling a day. Machinery had to be fenced off for safety. Factory inspectors were appointed.

1856 The first chemical dye, a brilliant mauve, was invented by W. H. Perkin. The dye was made from coal tar. It was soon followed by many others.

1874 Working hours for women and young people were lowered to 10 hours a day by law. Children up to 14 were to work only half a day.

1836 There was an enquiry into the punishment of two runaway apprentices called Esther Price and Lucy Garner. Power-looms were introduced for the first time and new weaving sheds were built.

1841 The last boy was taken on as an apprentice.

1894 Spinning was stopped at the mill since it no longer made enough money. Weaving carried on.

1904 The waterwheel suffered great damage and could not be repaired. It was scrapped and replaced by turbine engines.

1939 Quarry Bank Mill was given to the National Trust by Alec Greg, the great-great-grandson of Samuel Greg.

1959 Quarry Bank closed down.

1976 Work began to turn the mill into a museum.

1992 An official visit by the mill's patron, the Princess Royal.

Inside the factory

The great waterwheel installed at Quarry Bank in 1818 used a new type of gearing to transfer power over great distances. This modern wheel is a replacement, taken from another mill, but is similar to the original one.

The source of power at Quarry Bank Mill was water. The River Bollin ran fast enough to turn a waterwheel. The builders dug a channel called a mill race to divert the water over the wheel which drove the machinery through a system of gears and shafts.

Eventually, as the factory grew and technology improved, a huge iron suspension wheel was built. This could drive 10,000 spindles inside the factory. A steam engine was added as a back-up source of power when the water-level was low.

Cleaning and blending the raw cotton fibre

The carding process

Making strong yarn on a throstle spinner

Inside the factory, men, women and children laboured to feed the ever-turning machinery. The first job was to sort and blend the raw cotton. Once this had been done, the cotton was transferred to carding machines that straightened the cotton fibres, and turned them into long sausage shapes. Roving machines then drew out the cotton and added a loose twist. Finally, the rovings went to the spinning machines. Throstle spinners produced strong thread and mule spinners spun fine thread.

aking fine thread on a mule

These children are being shown how to make rovings by hand by Joe Carberry, an experienced factory worker. They are rolling the straightened fibres to make them ready for the spinning machine.

At first Quarry Bank produced only cotton thread but, as time passed, new weaving sheds were built and power-looms turned the thread into strong cotton cloth.

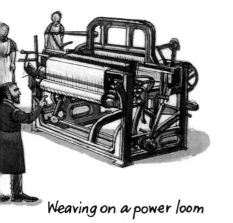

Weaving on a power loom

9

Who worked in the factory?

The children investigated the mill office where all the paperwork for the factory was done by the manager, the head book-keeper and two clerks. This girl examined one of the old mill ledgers to find out how much the workers were paid.

Quarry Bank Mill was deep in the country-side where the river was strong enough to drive the waterwheel. But the factory was far away from the nearest town and Samuel Greg found it hard to hire workers. To begin with, most spinners were suspicious of the factory. They were not used to going out to work and spending long hours looking after machinery.

Some workers walked to the factory from surrounding villages, but many came from further away. Whole families came from as far afield as London and Norfolk. The incomers had to sign documents agreeing to work at Quarry Bank six days a week for at least two years. Gradually, Samuel Greg enlarged the nearby village of Styal to house the new workers. He built cottages, a shop and a school

The 27 workers' cottages built by Samuel Greg in the village of Styal each had a kitchen, a parlour, two bedrooms, a cellar and an allotment. Rents were taken out of wages. The village shop was run by the mill Any workers who ran up bills had the money stopped from their wages.

There were jobs for men, women and children at the factory. The person in charge was the manager. Under him were engineers and mechanics who looked after the machinery. Overlookers, who checked that the carders and spinners were doing their jobs properly, were in charge of each section of the factory. At first there were no laws governing the age of workers or how long they worked. Women and children were quick, nimble-fingered and cheap to employ. Many jobs at Quarry Bank were done by children as young as nine.

A team of mechanics was employed to keep the machinery in good running order. At Quarry Bank they turned off the machines to do repairs, but in some factories the machines were left running. This caused lots of accidents.

The apprentices

In 1800 each town and village was expected to support its own orphans and poor children. But many councils, wishing to save themselves this expense, signed their poor children over to factory owners as cheap workers. About one-third of Samuel Greg's workers were 'pauper apprentices'.

Samuel Greg brought children to Quarry Bank from London and Liverpool. He said he preferred girls because they were less troublesome than boys. Greg built an Apprentice House to accomodate 100 child workers who were looked after by a superintendent and his wife.

The children brought a change of clothing and little else. They were expected to work up to 13 hours a day in exchange for food, clothing and somewhere to live. They had few comforts. Meals were very plain and they slept two to a bed in dormitories. Their free time was strictly controlled.

Apprentices usually had to stay at the factory for a period of seven years. Documents like this indenture promised that the factory owner would provide food, lodging, clothes and employment for them.

Today people can experience the life of an apprentice by joining in a 'living history' day at Quarry Bank Apprentice House. The children started by trying on clothes similar to those worn by apprentices.

When Quarry Bank Mill first started there were few rules about the treatment of child factory workers. But, as time passed, the government laid down laws to control hours of work and the amount of education that children should receive. In some factories apprentices were very badly treated. At Quarry Bank children were not cruelly treated, but their lives must have been very dreary.

Apprentices spent long hours doing boring jobs such as joining threads which had broken. This girl tried this on a spinning machine called a mule. She was surprised how hard it was to work quickly. Her fingers soon became stiff and sore.

Minding the machines

All day long the factory machinery ran at the same pace. The workers had to keep to the rhythm, feeding in the raw cotton and taking away the spun thread, however tired they were. They were constantly moving between machines, fetching and carrying, and trying to prevent breakdowns and hold-ups.

The apprentices did unskilled work such as changing bobbins, sweeping up, or carrying drums of cotton from the carders to the spinning machines. One job that needed speed and skill was that of the 'piecer' who followed the moving carriage of the spinning mule in and out, walking about 10 miles a day, while twisting the broken threads together.

The children tried out the apprentices' job of 'carrying the can' – moving a full drum of cotton rovings between one machine and another. They found that the cans were surprisingly heavy.

Working near moving machinery could lead to accidents. 'Scavengers' had one of the most dangerous jobs, as they cleaned fluff from underneath the moving machines. John Foden, an 11 year-old apprentice at Quarry Bank, had his head crushed by the returning carriage of the mule. Another apprentice, Thomas Priestley, described his work like this:

"I was set ...to attend two machines for spinning cotton, each of which spun 50 threads. My business was to supply these machines, to guide the threads ...also I learned to take the machinery to pieces and apply the oil, a matter that required some care."

Thomas lost a finger in this machine and, later, tried to run away.

This picture shows apprentices looking tired and miserable. A scavenger is underneath the mule. The factory owner is in the background. Pictures like this were used to gain public support for shorter working hours.

This girl is learning how to 'kiss the shuttle'. In early power-looms, the only way to thread a shuttle was to suck the yarn through a tiny hole. This task had to be repeated every few minutes. Workers who did this breathed in fibres of cotton which caused serious health problems.

Working conditions

The factory was a very noisy place. Machinery clattered and banged all day long, making it impossible to hear anyone speak. The air, kept hot and humid to prevent the thread from breaking in the machines, was thick with cotton dust.

The factory bell was used to call the workers. Discipline was hard and everyone had to work to a strict timetable.

These children are trying the clocking-in machine at the factory. They thought it was fun but factory workers were fined if they were late for work.

The factory had one shift of 13 hours starting at 6 am. There was a ten minute break for breakfast, half an hour for dinner and a further ten minutes for tea at the machines. Twice a week the dinner break was extended to an hour so the machines could be oiled. Overtime, or working longer hours, was often compulsory. For one week a year the factory was closed down for repairs and the workforce took a holiday. At all other times work never stopped.

Repeating the same task all day long and long hours of work could lead to injuries or even deformities in young children. Weekly pay was small – just a few pennies, mainly earned by overtime. In many cotton factories bad work was punished by brutal beatings. At Quarry Bank, fines were used.

Pay was worked out by the book-keeper and clerks in the factory office. It was taken round every week in these pay cups, minus any deductions for rent, shopping bought at the factory shop, or fines for poor work.

In 1836 two 16 year-old apprentices ran away from Quarry Bank. One of them, Esther Price, was caught, fined and locked up on her own. Her case received a lot of publicity, especially from supporters of the 'Ten Hour Movement' who wanted to reduce the hours that children worked.

Runaway apprentices were fined eight pence a day and girls might have their hair cut off. This girl is sitting where Esther Price was kept as a punishment after she ran away. The window was boarded up and she was given only porridge and bread to eat.

Home life

Samuel Greg built an Apprentice House a short distance from the factory to house the pauper children who worked for him. Visitors today can see for themselves what life must have been like for the 100 apprentices, and the husband and wife superintendents who lived there.

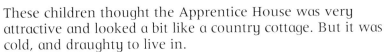
These children thought the Apprentice House was very attractive and looked a bit like a country cottage. But it was cold, and draughty to live in.

Samuel Greg believed that child apprentices should be hard-working and well-disciplined, and that they should grow up expecting very little. The apprentices were not cruelly treated, but their lives were very strictly controlled. They were allowed little freedom and almost no luxuries.

Today the house is furnished as it would have been 150 years ago, so that modern visitors can get a flavour of apprentice life. This child is finding out what it was like to do the chores under the watchful eye of the superintendent.

One apprentice wrote: "We were under the care of Richard Sims and his wife. The boys slept at one side of the house and the girls at the other... Our beds were good. We slept two to a bed and had clean sheets once a month".

In the Apprentice House there were no carpets or comfortable chairs, the dormitories were unheated and there were few toys to play with. Not that the children had much time to play after a 13-hour shift in the factory. They were expected to tend the vegetable garden, to fetch and carry, to chop sticks and draw water. Their only day of leisure was Sunday when they had to go to church both morning and afternoon.

Some apprentices did get into mischief. A number even ran away. But most apprentices accepted their lives without complaint. One apprentice called James Henshall worked at the factory for 44 years and eventually rose to become the manager.

Health and safety

Samuel Greg appointed Doctor Holland to look after the health and safety of the apprentices. The doctor visited them once a week and kept a record of his treatments. From his notebook the children discovered a great deal about the illnesses the apprentices suffered from.

These children chopped up horehound, a herb that was used to make cough mixture. Some of the remedies given to sick apprentices were not very effective, and most treatments consisted of herbal potions. Often leeches – small blood-sucking creatures – were used to suck out 'bad blood' when apprentices were ill.

There were many dangers to the health of children who worked in a factory. The heat, dust and noise caused eye complaints, breathing problems and deafness. Long hours and constant bending caused rheumatism and body deformities. Over the longer term, tuberculosis, cancer and lung disease caused many deaths.

This mixture of sulphur powder sweetened with black treacle was given regularly to 'clean out the system'. It tasted disgusting and was probably very bad for delicate stomachs.

There was constant danger from accidents with the machines. Loss of fingers was quite common, especially at the end of the day when the children were tired. In fact, accidents happened so often in factories that many people began to demand shorter working hours for women and children.

The government appointed inspectors to check working conditions and reduce the risk of injury. In 1833, inspectors heard that 17 apprentices died at Quarry Bank over a period of 22 years, one of them by an accident at the machinery.

The apprentices spent most of their lives in the dusty atmosphere of the factory but each had a patch of garden to look after which gave them the opportunity to get some fresh air.

Food and drink

For the apprentices at Quarry Bank, food and drink was plentiful but plain. Their diet consisted mainly of bread, porridge, milk and potatoes. Meat was a treat. Joseph Sefton, an apprentice in 1806, described his meals like this:

"On Sunday we had for dinner boiled pork and potatoes. We also had peas, turnips and cabbages in season. Monday we had for dinner milk and bread, sometimes thick porridge. We always had as much as we could eat. Tuesday we had milk and potatoes. Wednesday sometimes bacon and potatoes, sometimes milk and bread. Thursday if we had bacon on Wednesday we had milk and bread. Friday we used to have lobscouse (stew). Saturday we used to dine on thick porridge. We only had water to drink, when ill we were allowed tea."

The garden at the apprentice house supplied the household with vegetables. It was looked after partly by the apprentices themselves. Today the garden is run as a 'vegetable sanctuary', where old-fashioned varieties are grown in much the same way as they would have been 150 years ago. These children are helping to pick the runner bean crop.

Cooking was done on a kitchen range at the Apprentice House. Stodgy food like bread and porridge was the main fare. This boy is taking a wholemeal loaf out of the oven, watched by the 'superintendent', Ronan Brindley.

Breakfast and tea were eaten at the machines and usually consisted of bread or slabs of porridge. Anything sweet was a luxury and was eaten only at Sunday lunch when there might be a pudding. Christmas was the only time of year when treats such as buns and nuts were offered. We know that some apprentices were tempted to steal apples from local orchards. The ones who were caught were fined five shillings which they had to work off in overtime.

150 years ago food was not packaged the way it is today. This girl is trying to break pieces from a sugar loaf using a pair of sugar nippers. The apprentices were not given very much sweet food so it is unlikely that they would have been trusted with a job like this.

Clean and decent

The dormitories were swept and aired daily and the chamber pots emptied. These boys tried doing the sweeping. They found the brushes, which were made from twigs, left a lot of dust behind.

Samuel Greg believed that his apprentices were very well looked after. Their hours of work were long but they were decently clothed and fed. There were others who disagreed with this view and thought that the apprentice system was little more than slavery. But it was certainly true that conditions for the apprentices at Quarry Bank were cleaner and more comfortable than for many child workers who had to live in the overcrowded slums of Manchester.

The Apprentice House was kept clean and tidy at all times. The floors were swept and the rooms aired daily. Bed sheets were changed at least once a month and the walls were whitewashed every year to keep down bugs.

Few houses had running water at that time and Quarry Bank was no exception. The only source of water was an outside pump which supplied all the household needs for washing, cooking and cleaning. There were no bathrooms and indoor lavatories, but there were earth closets in the yard outside and chamber pots beneath the beds for night time use.

In the factory there were facilities for the workers to wash their hands and everyone was expected to be tidily dressed.

These children discovered that getting water from a pump is much harder than turning on a tap. Even when empty the wooden buckets were heavy. Full buckets needed two children to lift them.

The earth closet shown here is the forerunner of the flushing lavatory. A handful of earth was thrown down after use. Every so often the pit under the seat had to be cleaned out. This girl did not think much of the arrangement, but in fact it was quite hygienic.

Soap came in huge blocks like this. When soap was needed, smaller pieces had to be cut off the main block.

Nothing too fancy

The children tried on apprentice clothes to get the feel of life as young factory workers. They thought the apprentice clothes were much less comfortable than their own.

The apprentices had two sets of clothes, one for work and one for Sunday best. All the clothing was hard-wearing and sensible, with no allowances made for fashion. Anyone watching the apprentices walking to church on a Sunday morning would have known that they were poor children from the factory. One man described them like this:

"The girls were all dressed alike, their plain straw bonnets bound over the head with a green ribbon. The dresses were of stout cotton material though rather drab, a sort of fustian ... Woollen stockings and substantial shoes protected their feet. Cloaks protected them from the cold. Any lad that came sat apart. They wore corded breeches, woollen stockings and stout shoes. Jackets were of strong fustian, their high crowned hats were doffed on entering the church."

This boy tried a box iron. The core of metal was heated in the fire and dropped into the base of the iron with tongs or a hook. It was not as easy as modern-day ironing and people often burned themselves.

Washday was hard work, especially if there were 100 shirts to get clean. These children had a go with the dolly tub. The dolly churned the clothes in the water to loosen the dirt. Collars and cuffs had to be scrubbed with a soapy brush by hand.

When the children were working in the factory they wore their everyday clothes – plain dresses and aprons for the girls, breeches and shirts for the boys. Those who had to work at speed around the spinning mules often went barefoot, as this made them less likely to slip. The others wore heavy wooden clogs.

Working people usually wore heavy, strong footwear. Wooden-soled clogs like the one shown here were common in the factories.

Learning and leisure

When Quarry Bank first opened, all children did not have to go to school as they do today. The wealthy sent their children to school, but poor children were put to work as soon as possible. But in 1802, the government ruled that all factory children should receive some education during the working day. At Quarry Bank this took the form of classes after work.

Oak School in Styal village was built by Samuel Greg in 1823 for the factory workers' children. Apprentices attended evening classes after work. Today the school is still used by local children

Samuel Greg provided a schoolroom at the Apprentice House and employed a schoolmaster to take classes three nights a week between eight and nine o'clock. Reading, writing and mathematics were the main lessons. The boys benefitted most from them since the girls spent much of their school time learning to mend and sew. They were expected to make all their own clothes as well as shirts for the boys. Each year there was an Apprentice House Night when the best pupils were awarded prizes and buns.

The children found out that writing used to be a messy business with ink pots and quills! Apprentices were taught to write in a sloping style called 'copperplate'.

The Apprentice House schoolroom had sand trays like this one for the youngest children to learn their letters.

Samuel Greg's daughters also took an interest in the children's education. They taught needlework and Bible study on Sunday afternoons.

Leisure time was very restricted so there was little time for the apprentices to get into trouble. But we know they played games like marbles or bat and ball.

Ready-made clothes were not so common 150 years ago as they are today. It was thought essential for girls (but not boys) to be taught to sew as a preparation for thrifty adult life.

How to find out more

Visits

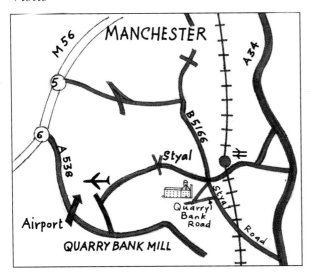

You can find out more about the history of the cotton industry by visiting Quarry Bank Mill where most of the pictures in this book were taken. You can visit the Apprentice House for a 'living history' experience of life as an apprentice at the beginning of the 19th century. The village of Styal has good examples of factory housing from the same period. Write for information about the mill to: Quarry Bank Mill, Styal, Cheshire SK9 4LA. Tel: 01625 527468.

Helmshore Textile Museum in Lancashire illustrates all aspects of the textile industry. Based in a restored fulling mill, it contains a collection of early textile machinery including a unique example of Arkwright's Water Frame. The address is: Helmshore Textile Museum, Holcombe Road, Helmshore, Rossendale, Lancashire BB4 4NP. Tel: 01706 226459.

New Lanark Mills is an example of a complete factory community based on cotton spinning. Run by Robert Owen, businessman and social reformer, it was a famous experiment in 'ideal' industrial living. The address is: The New Lanark Conservation Trust, New Lanark Mills, Lanark ML11 9DB. Tel: 01555 661345.

Things to do

Cat's cradle
Here is an old game to play with a length of yarn. Tie the ends together to make a big loop and put it over your hands. Follow these diagrams to make a 'cup and saucer'. Ask your parents if they can remember any other cat's cradle games to play.

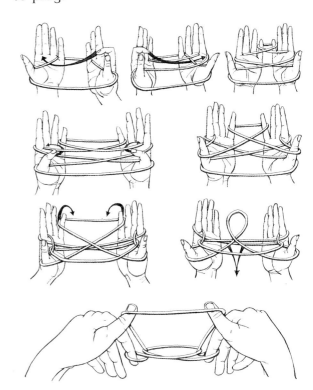

Make your own quill

The apprentices at Quarry Bank learned to write with a quill. Here is a cheat's way of making one.

You will need a large feather, an old biro, glue and a short piece of fuse wire. Take the biro to pieces and remove the inner tube of ink.
Snip off the end of the feather.
Bend the fuse wire in half and push it into the shaft of the feather to make it hollow. Push the ink tube into the shaft.

If it does not fit exactly, snip a bit off the end of the biro until it does. Seal the biro in place with a dab of glue at the neck.

Hand spinning

Yarn is spun by teasing and twisting the fibres of raw wool. The earliest method was with a drop spindle. Try it with sheep's fleece from a craft shop or picked from a fence near some grazing sheep.

1. Wash the wool to remove any dirt. Brush it between two hairbrushes to straighten the fibres. Roll it loosely into a roving.

2. Make a spindle using a pencil with a blob of modelling clay added to the bottom to give it weight.

3. Tie a strand of double knitting wool around the pencil tightly, leaving a loose end. Tease a little fibre from your roving and twist it on to the end of the knotted wool.

4. Spin the pencil and at the same time tease out more fibre from the roving. A twist will travel up the fibres and turn it into yarn.

When the spindle reaches the floor, wind the yarn on to it and then spin some more.

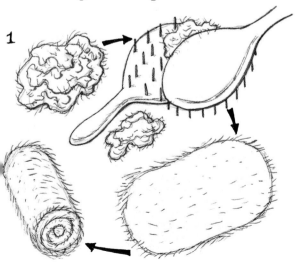

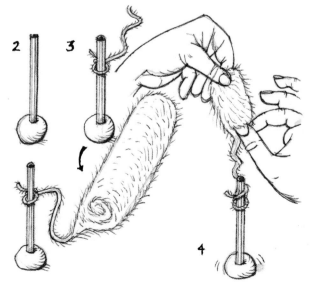

31

Index

First published 1996
A & C Black (Publishers) Limited
35 Bedford Row
London WC1R 4JH
ISBN 0-7136-4171-1

© 1996 A & C Black (Publishers) Limited

A CIP catalogue record for this book is available from the British Library

Acknowledgements
The author and publishers would like to thank the following people for their generous help:

Josselin Hill, Curatorial Director, Quarry Bank Mill Trust; Adam Daber, Assistant Curator; Christine Chadwick, Education Officer; Sarah Collins, Publicity Officer; Ronan Brindley and Sue Newby, Education Assistants at the Apprentice House; Mona Snape; Joe Carberry and all the staff at Quarry Bank Mill; Alexandra Smith, Mark Vesey, Robert Johnson, Beenish Javed, Sally Davies, Paul and Brenda Widger from the Bollin School, Atrincham; Vici Thompson and Rebecca Hopes from Puss Bank School, Macclesfield. And special thanks to Piers Gurney Ratcliff.

Photographs by Maggie Murray except for: p3 (left) Science and Society Picture Library; pp 2 ,4, 5, 8, 10, 11, 12, 15, 16 (right), 23 Quarry Bank Mill Trust Ltd.

Typeset in Meriden Infant 14/17pt

Printed and bound by Partenaires Fabrication, Malesherbes, France.